Virtual Friends

Helen Salter

Founder Editors: Bill Bowler and Sue Parminter

Illustrated by Monique Dong

Helen Salter has a degree in Modern Languages and has taught English in Paris. She works in the financial technology sector in London, and has written a number of books, including *The Summer Intern* in Oxford Bookworms and three teen fiction novels. This book was a delight to write because Paris is her favourite city. She lives in Surrey with her husband, two daughters, and the world's laziest cat.

OXFORD
UNIVERSITY PRESS

OXFORD
UNIVERSITY PRESS

Great Clarendon Street, Oxford, OX2 6DP, United Kingdom

Oxford University Press is a department of the University of Oxford.
It furthers the University's objective of excellence in research, scholarship,
and education by publishing worldwide. Oxford is a registered trade
mark of Oxford University Press in the UK and in certain other countries

ISBN: 978 0 19 424574 6   Book
ISBN: 978 0 19 462245 5   Book and Audio Pack

Printed in China

This book is printed on paper from certified and well-managed sources

ACKNOWLEDGEMENTS

Illustrations by: Monique Dong/The Bright Agency

The publisher would like to thank the following for their permission to reproduce photographs:
123RF pp4 (emoticons/oberart), 6 (Paris skyline at sunset/unknown1861), 7 (Notre Dame
cathedral and River Seine in Paris/Ivan Bastien), 12 (smartphone/tuntekron petsajun), 18
(laptop/Manit Khumrod), 35 (blue jeans/artqu), 35 (stain remover/George Tsartsianidis), 47
(smashed smartphone/rangizzz), 54 (graffiti/Engin Korkmaz), 54 (woman painting/Dmytro
Gilitukha), 54 (photo frame/Валентин Агапов), 56 (Paris flea market/Lembi Buchanan),
60 (Rio de Janeiro beach/ostill); Alamy Stock Photo pp (street art/guichaoua), 56 (Paris
river beach/eye35.pix); OUP pp (Eiffel Tower/Image Source), 26 (red umbrella/Mega Pixel),
60 (Mount Fuji, Japan/Sean Pavone), 60 (Tower Bridge, London/Medioimages), 60 (New
York City/upthebanner), 60 (Istanbul/Luciano Mortula); Shutterstock pp (Notre Dame
Catherdral/Neirfy), (Montmartre, Paris/T.W. van Urk), (Basilica Sacre Couer, Paris/Sailorr),
54 (explosion/Kuznetsov Alexey), 60 (Sagrada Familia, Barcelona/Rodrigo Garrido).

Contents

BEFORE READING

1 Match the people in the story with the sentences.

| *Violet's mum* | *Eline* | *Violet* | *Jess* | *Joy* |

1 . . . . just moved to Paris with her mum.

2 . . . . works for a make-up company.

3 . . . . and . . . . are sisters.

4 . . . . is Violet's best friend from London.

2 This story is in Paris. Which places do you think are in it? Tick the boxes.

The Eiffel Tower

Notre Dame

Montmartre

Les Frigos

Sacré-Cœur

1. In Paris

I watched Mum run up the stairs to our new flat. She was so excited!

I was not happy.

There was a **lift** in the building, but it was busy. The men helping us move were using it, mostly for light boxes of clothes. I was carrying heavy books and there were hundreds of stairs to climb.

'I liked our old house,' I said. 'I don't want to live in a flat.'

I tried not to be too unhappy this morning on the fast Eurostar train from London to Paris. But now I was tired and I couldn't hide it any more.

'We'll have the same number of rooms here as back home,' laughed Mum. 'But it will be wonderful. A real French flat! With big, tall windows! Look at these beautiful wooden stairs, Violet!'

lift this takes people to different floors in a building

Mum loves Paris. Really loves it. Just because she lived here when she was a student, about a hundred years ago.

It was so **annoying**.

'A flat won't feel right, with the kitchen on the same floor as the bedrooms,' I said.

'I'm sure you'll learn to like it,' smiled Mum. 'It'll be a great home.'

'It will never be home,' I said and I put down my box. 'Wait – I feel ill. We're too high up. The **air** is too thin! I can't live here.'

Mum turned to give me a look. 'Fourteen and in Paris! What an adventure!'

'Yes,' I thought to myself, 'But we're very different.'

Mum looked at my face and said, 'Wait until you're an adult and you need to work. Sometimes you have to make difficult **decisions**.'

'Oh, good,' I thought. 'The Difficult Decisions conversation again.' I **picked up** my box. Back home in London, I always felt that something would go wrong. Firstly, I thought that Starlight Cosmetics would change their decision and not give Mum the **marketing** job in their Paris office. Mum did the marketing in London. It was her job to give the **make-up** great names so people wanted to buy it. She loved her job.

Then, I thought that the teachers at my old school would say, 'Violet can't leave! All her friends are here and they really like her!' But when I told the teachers where I was going, they all said I was going to have a wonderful time.

I didn't think so. At home, it was easy to be myself. My friends all liked the same things as me. In the evenings, we all sent **messages** on our phones. At the weekend, we went shopping and talked for hours. Here, Mum wanted me to be excited all the time because I was in Paris. But Paris meant nothing without the right people. To me, Paris was a stupid place full of buildings that all looked the same. People thought it was beautiful and special. But it was just old and boring.

annoying not nice; something that you want to stop happening

air we take this in through our mouth and nose

decision a thing that you have to choose

pick up to start carrying something

marketing helping to sell the things a company makes

make-up something that you put on your face to look good

message you write this to someone and send it with your phone or computer

I arrived at the door of the new flat for the first time and went inside. I didn't look around. I sat on the big, comfortable chair from home – it was the first thing the men took upstairs. I quickly got my phone from my pocket and began to think about my friends in London. I felt sure that Jess wasn't in bed yet, and Ruby, Danielle, and Lara were watching TV as usual.

Mum saw me and looked unhappy. She didn't like it when I spent time on my phone. But I needed to use it more now, didn't I?

Oh, good! I already had not one, or two, but seven messages!

Jess's message was a photo of herself. She was next to an empty seat outside the shops in town. She looked really unhappy. Underneath, it said, 'I'm so lonely. 😢'

For a second, I felt better. Jess was my best friend, and we had plans for a holiday in Spain this summer with her family. Mum said I could fly there from Paris!

I'm so lonely 😢

I quickly took a photo of myself in the new flat and sent it to everyone with the words, 'We have arrived. Bad luck to me. 😢'

About five seconds later, there was a message from Jess. 'WHY AREN'T YOU HERE? 😢'

'My phone is the answer,' I thought to myself. 'I'll be there with my friends, just **virtually**. I'll still send messages! I'll still show people my photos! Nothing will change!'

'Come and see your room, Violet!' said Mum. She was carrying her big light. She bought it before we came to Paris because she got excited in the shop and thought it looked French. I told her the lights in France would be more French, but she didn't listen to me.

'You can see lots of interesting buildings from your window,' said Mum.

virtual not real, not really there

'I'll look in a minute,' I said.

She smiled at the man helping us move. He smiled back. Men always think my mum is wonderful. I don't know why. She's really untidy and she can't cook.

When I didn't move, Mum said, 'You can take your things out of your boxes before we go out!'

'Go out where?' I asked.

'I told you on the train!' said Mum. 'There's a party at the **international** school. So you can meet the other students during the summer, before school starts in September.'

'I don't need more friends,' I said. 'I have friends already.'

'Yes, but new friends are good, too,' smiled Mum. 'Ones that are in the same country.'

I showed her my phone. 'This is all I need,' I said.

She laughed.

But I wasn't **joking**.

international to do with many countries

joke to say something funny

5

READING CHECK

Match the first and second parts of these sentences.

a Violet says that Paris

b Violet liked her old house and says she

c Violet's mum is excited about

d Violet's mum works at Starlight Cosmetics

e People think Paris is beautiful and special

f Violet's mum wants Violet to go to the party

1 living in Paris.

2 to meet new friends.

3 but Violet thinks it is old and boring.

4 doesn't want to live in a flat.

5 and has a new job in Paris.

6 will never be her home.

WORD WORK

1 Complete the crossword with eight new words from Chapter 1.

2 Use the words from Activity 1 to complete the sentences.

a People who live in tall buildings often use a ....lift........ instead of the stairs.

b There are people at Starlight Cosmetics from Europe, America, and Asia – it is a very .... place.

c I'd like to have a job in .... one day so I can help a company sell the things it makes.

d People send each other billions of .... every day on the internet.

e Choosing which city to live in is a very difficult ....

f It is very .... when your mum asks you to put down your phone.

g Starlight Cosmetics makes lots of different .... – there is something for everyone.

h Violet and her friends are not together any more but they can still be .... friends on the Internet.

GUESS WHAT

Which of these things do you think happen in the next chapter? Tick the boxes.

	Yes	No
a Violet goes home to London.	☐	☐
b Jess comes to Paris.	☐	☐
c Violet's mum decides she wants to live in China.	☐	☐
d Violet throws her phone in the river.	☐	☐
e Violet meets some new people at the party.	☐	☐

2. The international school

'Look at that person over there,' said Mum when we arrived. 'She's all alone. Perhaps she needs a new friend.'

'Mum,' I said, 'I think that's a teacher.'

This was so **embarrassing**. We were standing in a big room at the international school, with lots of other students. OK, there were lots of other mothers there too, but they weren't embarrassing. They didn't want their children to talk to new people all the time. I thought that most **parents** didn't want their children to speak to strangers?

Mum saw a table with drinks on it. 'Violet, let's have a drink.'

I went with her, but only because I didn't want to stand there alone.

I took the last orange **juice**, just before someone arrived at the table.

'Oh!' she said.

'Sorry,' I said. 'Would you like this drink?'

'No, it's OK,' she said. 'Are you new?'

'Yes,' I said. 'Well, I start in Year Ten in September.'

'I'll be in Year Ten, too!' she said. 'Hi. I'm Eline.'

embarrassing
when something or someone makes you feel worried about what other people think of you

parents mother and father

juice a drink made from fruit

Why did I think I knew her? Oh – she looked like Maisie Bickford from school! She had the same blue eyes and long yellow hair. Jess didn't like Maisie because she was always so happy about everything.

Jess sometimes secretly sent me a message on her phone during **science** lessons. 'It's Monday morning. WHY IS SHE SMILING?'

Jess had to work with Maisie in science because our teacher, Mr Chan, liked to decide who you worked with. You couldn't work with your best friend. He said some people talked too much if they worked together. (He always looked at Jess and me when he said this.)

OK, I knew Eline and Maisie were different people, but they looked nearly the same. And Eline was just like another person, too. Who was it?

'Hello!' said my mum, smiling at her.

'Hello!' said Eline.

She was just like my mum! Eline sounded really **positive** all the time, just like her.

science the study of the natural world

positive always happy about things

9

'Are you new, too?' said Mum. I **pretended** I didn't know what she meant.

'No, I've been here a year. But I still remember being new at the school,' said Eline. 'My little sister Joy and I moved here from Norway.'

'Isn't Paris wonderful?' said Mum.

'Oh, yes!' cried Eline. They both looked at me.

'Sorry,' I said. 'I like London.'

They both began talking about how great Paris was and where the best food markets were. I stopped listening. Then suddenly I heard Mum say, 'Oh – we live really near you, then! Come to the flat and play with Violet sometime!'

It was like I was five years old or something.

'Mum,' I said quickly, 'I don't need anyone to come to the flat and play – I'm not a baby. And I'm going to Spain soon to see Jess!'

Eline **paused** for a second, then smiled. 'Well, it was nice to meet you. Goodbye.'

On the walk home, Mum said to me, 'The school is planning a **picnic** soon. It will be a great way to meet more new people.'

'I don't need to meet anyone new,' I said. Again. Perhaps I needed to write it on a piece of paper and hold it up every time Mum spoke to me.

'OK, OK,' said Mum. 'I just thought there would be some nice people there.'

Suddenly, I thought of something. Before I left, Jess told me, 'Your mum doesn't like me.'

'Yes, she does!' I told her.

'No,' said Jess. 'She doesn't. This Paris thing? It's just to stop us being friends.'

'No!' I said to Jess at the time.

But now Mum was pushing me to meet new people, and I wasn't so sure. But perhaps it was too much. I mean, changing

pretend to try to make somebody believe something that is not true

pause to stop for a second

picnic a meal that people eat outside, often sitting on the ground

10

house, changing job, changing country. Other parents just took away their children's phones.

'Oh, my phone,' I thought suddenly.

I picked it up and – no internet.

'No internet!' I said to Mum.

'Oh no!' she said. She was possibly not as unhappy as me. 'You'll have to look at this wonderful bridge **instead**.'

I looked up. We were crossing a bridge over a big river. Great. I looked back down at my phone. Oh, Jess was **online**!

'Boring party,' I wrote. It was difficult to write because we were now walking on **cobbles**. Trying to walk and send messages to your friends is very dangerous. But, I was OK – I knew how to do it.

'Have you got a new best friend?' replied Jess.

'Yes,' I wrote. 'Her name is Eline and she's just like Maisie, but even more boring.'

'How is that possible?' wrote Jess.

Was she in her garden right now? We always sat outside by her kitchen door at this time of day, just before dinner.

'She loves Paris, like my mum!' I wrote.

'Tell her she's boring. Or leave her at the top of the **Eiffel Tower**,' said Jess.

'Ha!' I said aloud.

'What?' said Mum.

'Nothing,' I said.

instead in place of

online when you are on the internet

cobbles small stones used for making streets

Eiffel Tower /ˈaɪfəl ˈtaʊər/ a very famous, tall building in Paris

READING CHECK

Are these sentences true or false? Tick the boxes.

		True	False
a	Violet's mum tells her not to talk to anyone at the school party.	☐	☑
b	Violet is really happy to be at the party.	☐	☐
c	Violet doesn't know anyone at the international school.	☐	☐
d	Eline looks like Jess.	☐	☐
e	Eline is a positive person.	☐	☐
f	Eline has a little brother called Sam.	☐	☐
g	The school is planning a picnic soon.	☐	☐
h	Violet tells Jess that Eline is boring.	☐	☐

WORD WORK

1 Find words from Chapter 2 in the messages.

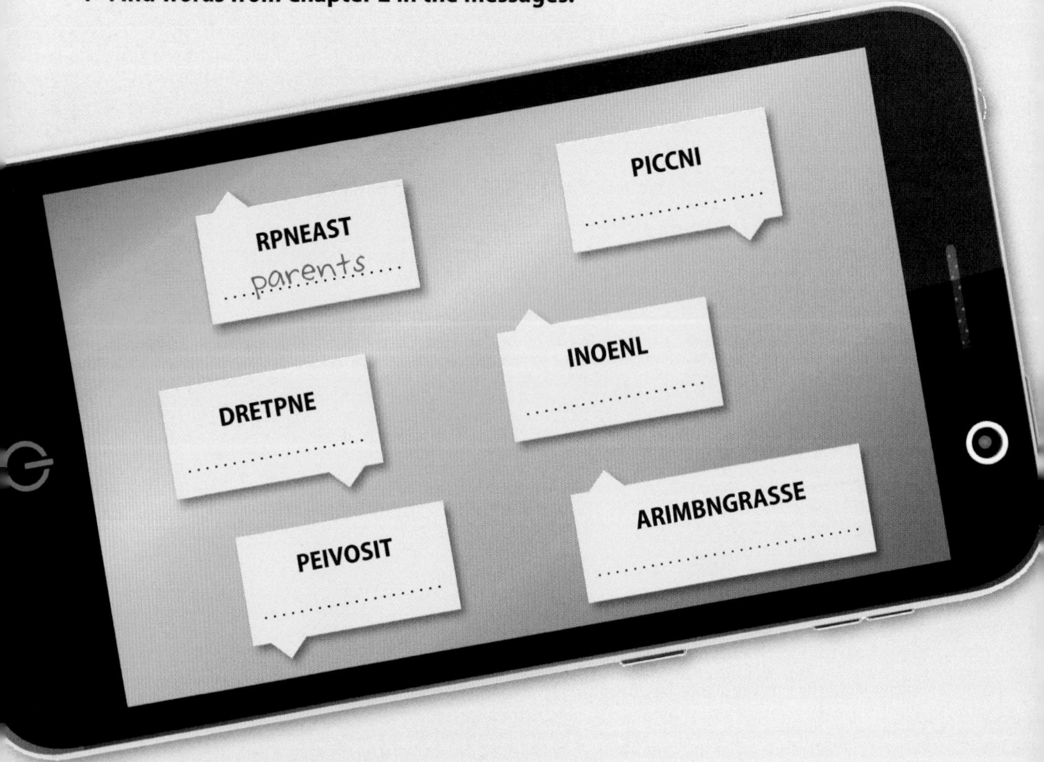

PICCNI

RPNEAST
...parents...

INOENL

DRETPNE

ARIMBNGRASSE

PEIVOSIT

12

2 Fill in Violet's diary with the words from Activity 1.

Today we went to the international school party. Everyone was there with their …parents… . Mum wanted me to make new friends. It was so ………………! Why is she so ……………… and happy all the time, when I feel terrible? Mum wants us to go to the international school ……………… too. Maybe I will ……………… to be ill and not go!

I met a girl called Eline today. She was OK, but boring. I am so happy that I can still send messages to Jess ………………!

GUESS WHAT

Which of these things do you think happen in the next chapter? You can tick more than one.

1 Violet…
- **a** ☐ goes to the picnic.
- **b** ☐ looks at her phone a lot.
- **c** ☐ goes shopping with Eline.
- **d** ☐ tells Jess she doesn't want to be her friend any more.

2 Violet's mum…
- **a** ☐ says that she doesn't like Eline and Joy.
- **b** ☐ tells Violet that Paris is wonderful.
- **c** ☐ doesn't listen to Violet.
- **d** ☐ buys a kitten for Violet.

3 Eline…
- **a** ☐ climbs up the Eiffel Tower.
- **b** ☐ goes back to Norway.
- **c** ☐ sends a message to Jess.
- **d** ☐ gives Violet's mum a big hug.

4 Jess…
- **a** ☐ goes shopping.
- **b** ☐ eats lots of chocolate.
- **c** ☐ tells Violet that she misses her.
- **d** ☐ sends Violet's mum an email.

3. A long message

'What's it about?' I asked, looking at the TV.

'I told you,' said Mum from the **sofa**. 'It's a film about a girl in Paris.'

It was the end of Mum's second week in her new job. She was wearing her oldest clothes, which meant she was tired.

'Is it in French?' I asked.

She paused then said, 'Yes, but there are the English words underneath.'

'Great,' I thought. Was this my life now? Usually on a Friday night, I was at Jess's house. Later, we met the others at the cinema or went for pizza. Her parents drove us there and back. Now, I was in the wrong country for cinema or pizza, and the only thing for me to do was watch a film with my mum. A film in the wrong language.

Mum looked at the empty sofa next to her. 'I've got some chocolate,' she said.

OK. Well, I was hungry. I sat down and began watching the film. Or reading it.

It was about a girl in Paris who was always happy. Mum looked at me a lot during the film. I knew what she was thinking. She wanted to see me suddenly fall in love with Paris, run outside, then jump up and down happily. Instead, she saw me smile when my phone **beeped**.

It was a photo of what Jess was wearing tonight! She sent it to all our friends. Then Ruby, Danielle, and Lara posted photos, too. So, they were all going out somewhere?

I sent Jess a message. 'You look nice! Is that a new coat?'

'Jess has got a new coat,' I told Mum.

'Good for her,' said Mum. She was still watching the film. She didn't **care** about anything.

'It's not good,' I said. I suddenly felt angry. 'Everyone is going out and I'm here, doing nothing! They go out all the time. And

sofa a long comfortable seat for people to sit on together

beep to make a small noise

care to feel interested in, and to worry about, someone or something

their lives are really **cool**.'

cool really great

'Their lives are not really cool,' said Mum. 'No one's life is as wonderful as it looks online. People only show you the photos they look good in. You never see the boring pieces of their life, do you? They never show you pictures of themselves in the car on the way to their grandmother's house, or washing their face, or in a science lesson.'

I thought about the time when Jess took photos in a science lesson. She wanted to see if her hair looked OK. But Mr Chan took away her phone.

Beep!

I had a reply from Jess!

It said, 'Yes, I bought it today. Danni was looking for a hat, but she didn't find one. But I saw the coat and Danni said it looked really cool!'

'Jess went shopping with Danielle?' I thought to myself.

'Jess went shopping with Danielle,' I told Mum.

'Good for her,' said Mum. She was still watching the film.

'Then an **elephant** sat on her head,' I said.

'Good for her,' said Mum.

It was possible that she wasn't listening.

I looked at Mum. She was happily watching Paris in the film. Mum looked **pretty** from here. Mum was old, but people always said she was pretty.

Poor Jess. She had to go shopping with Danielle? She pretended to like her when we were all together. But when we were alone, she said that Danielle was really boring and talked too much.

After I went to bed, I thought of something: Jess didn't **actually** say in her message that it was terrible shopping without me. She meant to say it, I was sure. She just forgot.

Five minutes later, I sat up in bed and picked up my phone. I paused for a minute. I heard Mum turn over in her bed in the next room. Perhaps she wasn't asleep yet. Could she hear me? She didn't like me using my phone at night. She told me yesterday that she wasn't sleeping very well because her new bed was uncomfortable.

I began writing a quick message to Jess, but soon it was a really long message. It was great! I told her all about my day. I asked lots of questions about her shopping and where she went and what they all did. I read it all the way through before I sent it.

elephant a very big animal with a long nose

pretty beautiful

actually truly; what really happens

Half an hour later, I put down my phone. My eyes hurt a little, but I felt better. Now Jess knew that being friends was still important to me. And, it didn't matter how many times Jess had to go shopping with boring Danielle, we were still best friends.

READING CHECK

Correct the mistakes in these sentences.

1 Violet and her mum watch a film about a girl in ~~London.~~ *Paris*

2 Violet's mum is sitting on the floor.

3 At home, Violet liked to go to the museum on a Friday night.

4 Violet shares a photo of what she is wearing.

5 Jess has a new bag.

6 Violet thinks her friends' lives are terrible.

7 Violet's mum says that people share the boring bits of their lives online.

8 Jess went swimming with Danni.

9 Violet sends Jess a very short message.

WORD WORK

1 Find the words from Chapter 3 on the screen:

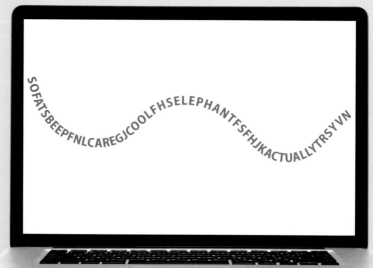

SOFATSBEEPFNLCAREGJCOOLFHSELEPHANTFSFHJKACTUALLYTRSYVN

2 Match words from Activity 1 with the pictures.

a ....

b ....

c ....

d ....

GUESS WHAT

What happens next? Tick three boxes.

1 ☐ Jess sends Violet an even longer message.
2 ☐ Violet watches the film again and decides she loves Paris.
3 ☐ Jess doesn't get Violet's message.
4 ☐ Violet goes to the international school picnic with her mum.
5 ☐ Violet's mum takes away her phone
6 ☐ Violet sees Eline again.
7 ☐ Violet's mum has a big surprise for Violet.

4. The picnic

'What time is it?' I asked sleepily.

'It's 11 a.m.,' said Mum. She shook me excitedly, then left the room. She called, 'I'll give you five minutes, Violet. But then we need to go, OK?'

Oh! I remembered. It was the international school picnic today. I got up and looked out of the window.

'I think it's going to rain,' I said.

'Don't be stupid!' said Mum.

An hour later, we were sitting in a small park in the north-east of Paris. Most people had paper bags with their food in, but Mum had a **picnic basket**. I had an **umbrella** with me. In England it rained a lot. Jess always carried one, because she was worried about her hair. Jess!

I got out my phone and looked at it. 'What is the matter?' I thought to myself. There was no reply from Jess to my message! My special, long message! Did it send? I looked. Yes, it sent at 11.30 p.m. last night. But there was no reply from Jess.

I moved the phone around to see if it was possible to get messages, and then I heard a voice.

'Hi, Violet!'

'Oh, hi, Eline.'

She was wearing a red dress and holding a camera. 'Smile!' she said. Mum and I smiled for the photo.

'You both look very English,' said Eline. 'A picnic basket and an umbrella!'

I smiled again, but I was thinking, 'What happened to Jess?'

Perhaps she replied, but her message was so long that it crashed the internet. That's why it didn't arrive. Or perhaps Mum came into my room at night, took my phone and **blocked** all calls and messages from England?

'Mum, did you come into my room last night and block all messages from England?' I asked.

picnic basket a special box for carrying picnic food

umbrella a thing that you hold over your head to keep you dry when it rains

block to stop from arriving

Mum laughed. 'Don't be stupid!' Then she paused and said, 'Why, can you do that?'

'No, I was only joking,' I said quickly. She sounded interested. Mum wanted me to turn off my phone and run around Paris saying, 'Wow! This is beautiful!'

'Are you OK?' asked Eline. She sat down next to us.

'I'm fine,' I said. 'But my best friend hasn't replied to a message I sent last night.'

'I remember leaving my friends in Norway,' said Eline. 'It was really bad at first.'

'I know!' I said. Mum didn't hear her, which was annoying.

'Don't worry,' said Eline. 'It's a different time in England.'

Yes! Eline was right. Perhaps Jess was still asleep!

I smiled at Eline. Perhaps I was wrong about her. She was nice.

For the first time in Paris, I looked around. It was a pretty park. It was a sunny day, but not too hot. Perhaps I didn't need the umbrella. I lay on my back and closed my eyes.

Eline lay on her back too. 'I've got some nice French bread for the picnic,' she said. 'I feel hungry already.'

'Do you **miss** the food in Norway?' I asked.

'No,' laughed Eline.

'I miss English food,' I said. I shut my eyes, but suddenly I heard my phone beep! I jumped up and picked up my phone. What? There was nothing there!

'That happens a lot,' said Eline. 'You think you can hear your phone, because you want to get a message. But there's nothing there.'

Eline was being nice.

'Come and meet my sister, Joy,' she said. She stood up. 'And I know lots of other people here, too.'

'That's really kind of you,' I said. 'Can I come and meet them in five minutes?'

'OK!' said Eline. She walked away.

'Why didn't you go with Eline?' asked Mum.

'I just didn't,' I said. I quickly wrote, 'Jess, are you online?' and hit Send.

But there was no reply.

'Violet, please try to enjoy yourself here, now,' said Mum.

She sounded annoyed. 'You're in Paris and you aren't even happy to be here! Look, you can see **Sacré-Cœur** behind those trees!'

'So what?' I said. 'Places don't make you happy, do they? People make you happy. And all my friends are in London.'

I sent Jess another message: 'HELLO???'

Then I saw something and I felt ill. I saw a message online from Jess to Lara. She sent it five minutes ago! She wasn't asleep. She was online! She just didn't want to reply to me!

After that, the rest of the picnic was terrible. Mum wanted me to go and say hello to Eline's sister Joy. She looked just like Eline, but three years younger. When I saw Eline with her sister and her friends, I missed Jess even more. So I went back to Mum, sat down next to her, put up my umbrella, and hid under it.

'What are you doing? It's sunny,' said Mum.

'I know,' I told her.

On the way home, I walked behind Mum and tried not to cry.

When we were nearly home, Mum waited and then tried to look under the umbrella. I had to stop really quickly so I didn't crash into her.

'Violet?' she said.

'It's going to rain, OK?' I said. Then I started crying, a lot. It was **probably** the first time ever that it was wetter inside an umbrella than outside.

Mum paused then said, 'Violet, I know you miss Jess, OK? This was a surprise, but perhaps I'll tell you now.'

What was she talking about? I closed the umbrella to look at her. I dried my face with one hand.

Mum said, 'Jess is coming to visit you in Paris!'

'What?' I said.

'She's coming next weekend!' she explained. 'So, you'll see her before you both go to Spain in September! She's getting the Eurostar. I'll put another bed in your room.'

Sacré-Cœur
/sakʁe kœʁ/
a big, famous church on a hill in Paris

probably almost certainly true

23

Oh! Suddenly, I felt really happy. Jess was coming to Paris! So, that was why she didn't reply! She didn't want to tell me about the surprise! For the first time in Paris, I gave Mum a big **hug**.

'Be careful with that umbrella!' said Mum, but I could tell she was pleased.

'Quick, let's go back to the flat,' I said. 'I really need to tidy my room!'

That evening, after my room was ready, I went into the living room. Mum was sitting at the table looking at some make-up. She looked tired.

'What are you doing?' I asked. Mum didn't like working at the weekend.

'I need to think of names for this new make-up by Monday,' said Mum. She held up a Starlight Cosmetics **nail polish**. 'Great Green?'

'I don't think so,' I said.

'What about these?' asked Mum. 'Perfect Pink? Beautiful Brown?'

I laughed. 'I don't know,' I said. I wasn't very good at thinking of **ideas**. Suddenly, the phone rang in the living room.

I picked up the phone. 'Hello?'

'Hello,' said a strange voice. 'It's Eline.'

'Oh, hello!' I said.

hug when you put your arms around someone

nail polish special paint for the ends of your fingers

idea a plan or a new thought

24

'I got your number from the names of the people going to the picnic. I'm just phoning to see if you're OK. You were unhappy earlier, about your friend.'

'Oh! How embarrassing,' I thought. 'That was all just a stupid mistake.'

'No, no, I'm fine,' I said quickly. 'Sorry. Thanks for calling. But everything is OK now. Jess, my best friend, is coming to see me this weekend! It was a surprise!'

'That's great!' said Eline. She sounded pleased. 'You'll have to take her to the Eiffel Tower. And will you go to Sacré-Cœur? It's so quiet and dark inside. It feels special.'

'Yes, probably!' I said. I didn't have any plans yet. I didn't know any good places in Paris.

'And there are some great markets,' said Eline. 'Shall we meet up? Joy and I can show you some of our favourite places, if you like?'

'OK!' I said, without really thinking about it.

'Great! I'll phone you on Friday,' said Eline.

'OK,' I said and I put down the phone. My idea was to spend the whole weekend with Jess. But now there were plans to see Eline and Joy, too. 'It's all right,' I said to myself. 'Jess will be OK with that. And Eline will love Jess. Everyone likes her. Jess is so cool!'

READING CHECK

Match the first and second parts of these sentences.

a Violet's mum tells her she has to get out of bed because

b Violet is unhappy at the picnic because

c Eline calls Violet and offers to show

d Violet's mum is annoyed because

1 Violet is on her phone at the picnic.

2 when she starts to cry.

3 it's the international school picnic today.

4 Violet starts to think perhaps she was wrong about her.

e Violet is walking under her umbrella

f Violet is really happy because

g Eline is nice to Violet, and

h Violet is surprised when

5 Eline phones to ask if she is OK.

6 she does not have a message from Jess.

7 Jess is coming to Paris!

8 her and Jess some good places in Paris.

WORD WORK

Choose the right word for these sentences using the words in the umbrella.

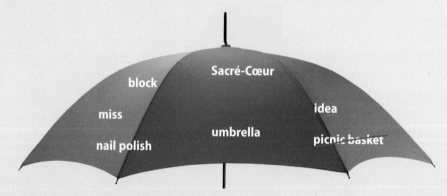

block   Sacré-Cœur   idea   miss   umbrella   nail polish   picnic basket

a I'm going to a picnic. I will take a *picnic basket* / *kitchen*.

b It's raining so I need my *newspaper* / *umbrella*.

c I received a message from someone I don't know, and I want to *block* / *kiss* it.

d If I am away from my family, I *watch* / *miss* them.

e There is a big church in Paris called *the Eiffel Tower* / *Sacré-Cœur*.

f My sister loves *nail polish* / *hamburgers*; her fingernails are always different colours!

g The party is 5 kilometres away. It was not a good *idea* / *surprise* to walk!

GUESS WHAT

**Who does what in the next chapter? Match the names with the sentences.
You can use each name more than once.**

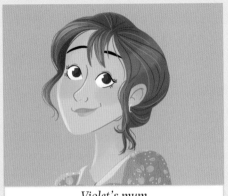

Violet's mum

Violet

Jess

Eline & Joy

a .... comes to Paris for the weekend.

b .... is very happy to see Jess!

c .... is happy because Violet is not sad any more.

d .... spend some time with Violet and Jess.

e .... has an extra bed in her room for the weekend.

f .... takes lots of photos of her weekend in Paris.

g .... show Violet and Jess their flat.

5. A great weekend

'And this is our flat,' I told Jess. 'Look, you can see the Eiffel Tower!' It was great. Jess was here, in Paris!

Mum laughed. She went into the kitchen and called, 'Jess, that's the first time Violet has ever talked about the Eiffel Tower.'

Jess made a funny face. I laughed. It was so good to have someone here who knew me, the real me. We had plans to look round Paris today, and later to visit Eline and Joy for dinner at their flat, five minutes away. There was a second bed in my room for Jess. Jess and I always talked all night!

We spent the day visiting famous places in Paris. We went up the river in one of the boats. It was my idea! We didn't have to walk everywhere with hundreds of other visitors.

Jess took lots of photos and told me everything that was happening back home. She said that Lara bought a hat that Danni wanted. Danni wanted the hat more, but Lara said she saw it first. So now Danni wasn't talking to Lara any more.

'Is Danni still really boring?' I asked. I knew it wasn't very nice to say that, but I needed to hear that Jess missed me, just a little.

But Jess said, 'Oh – look at that building!' And she got out her phone.

'Wait a second,' I said. 'My hair looks untidy because of the wind.'

'Oh – that's OK,' said Jess. She looked into her phone, smiled, and took about a hundred photos of herself. She moved the phone a little each time.

'Each picture has to be different,' she explained, 'So I'll always look good in one of them.'

'Would you like a photo of both of us?' I asked, but Jess put her phone away. Suddenly, we went under a bridge. For a minute, it was really cold in the **shadows**. But soon we were back in the sun.

Later, we got ready to go to Eline and Joy's flat.

'Does your mum still get lots of free make-up with her job? Can I have some nail polish?' asked Jess. She picked up my make-up bag.

'Yes,' I said.

It was so nice to see her. We looked at all our clothes and talked about what to wear.

Then we walked to Eline and Joy's flat. We went up in the lift and Eline met us on the fourth floor.

'Hi, Eline,' I said. 'This is my best friend, Jess.'

'Hi, Jess,' said Eline. 'I'm Eline. This is Joy.'

'Hello!' said Jess. Then, she said to me in a quiet voice, 'You were right. She looks just like Maisie!'

'Sorry?' said Eline to Jess.

'Nothing,' replied Jess, and she smiled at me.

'Oh no!' I thought to myself. 'I forgot I said that about Eline.'

shadow a dark shape that the sun makes on things

29

We walked into Eline and Joy's flat. The walls in the living room were a pretty yellow colour and there was a nice smell of cooking from the kitchen. There was wooden furniture everywhere and a white square of carpet on the floor.

I saw some great pictures on the walls. There were two photos, both of cobbles with shadows across them.

'Are these your photos?' I asked Eline. I remembered her holding a camera at the picnic.

'Yes!' said Eline.

'Look at these wonderful pictures!' I told Jess. I wanted everyone to talk happily!

'Oh, I like taking pictures, too!' Jess told Eline. 'Well, photos of myself, mostly. Maybe you can take some photos of me while I'm here?'

Suddenly, there was a loud voice from the kitchen. 'Dinner's ready!'

Eline and Joy's dad came out of the kitchen. He was drying his hands. 'Enjoy it, girls! I'll leave you alone to talk.' He left the room.

'He's going to watch TV in the other room,' said Eline. Then she said, 'I haven't met your dad yet, Violet. Does he work a lot?'

Jess went very quiet.

'Er, my dad died when we were still living in London,' I said. 'He was riding his bicycle to work. A car hit him.'

Eline looked at Joy. 'Oh no!' said Eline. 'I'm so sorry. Was it a long time ago?'

'Not really,' I said. 'Last year.'

Eline and Joy just looked at me with their big blue eyes. I wanted Jess to start a different conversation, but she didn't say anything.

'Shall we eat?' I asked.

The food was really nice, but Jess didn't finish it. She talked a lot instead.

After the meal, I said to Eline, 'We've brought you some chocolates to say thank you. They're from London.'

'Oh, thank you!' said Eline. 'They'll be really good, then. I know that everything about London is really cool!'

Jess looked at me, then laughed loudly.

'What?' I said.

'Is that what you've said?' she laughed. 'You hated London!'

'I did not!' I said.

'Yes, you did,' said Jess. 'You **complained** about it all the time.'

'I did not!' I replied. 'I loved it!'

'You complain about everything because you're so **negative**!' said Jess.

'I'm an **optimist**!' I said, a little annoyed. But everyone was laughing.

'Violet, you are not,' said Jess.

I didn't like this conversation. Yes, I wanted everyone to be friends. But I didn't want them all to laugh at me.

'You haven't said anything good about anyone since you arrived here!' said Jess.

'OK, stop talking!' I thought. But Jess didn't look at me.

complain to say that you are unhappy or angry about something

negative when a person always thinks or says bad things

optimist a person who always thinks or says positive, good things

'Not even good things about us?' laughed Eline.

'Don't worry,' said Jess. 'Violet thinks everyone is boring. Not just you.'

Suddenly the room was silent. No one was laughing any more.

I looked at Jess to see if she wanted to say sorry, but she didn't! She just drank her drink.

'Sorry,' I said quickly. 'What Jess means is…'

'Don't worry!' said Eline brightly. 'I'm sure we're not that interesting. Would you like some more **grape** juice?'

Suddenly I felt terrible. Why did Jess say that? But I knew it was my **fault**, too. I told Jess that Eline was boring.

grape a small purple or green fruit

fault when something bad happens because of you

'I'd love some more juice,' I said quietly. I stood up. Eline picked up the grape juice but it was very heavy and she **spilled** some over Jess!

'My jeans!' cried Jess.

'Oh no, the carpet!' I said. There was dark juice on the beautiful white carpet! I tried to clean it quickly, but Jess was still talking about her jeans. In the end, Joy gave Jess some water to put on her jeans, and then Eline helped me to clean the carpet.

'I'll do it. Don't worry,' said Eline. But she wasn't looking at me.

'Violet, we must go now!' said Jess. She was still trying to clean her jeans. 'These are new!' she said. 'I'll have to **soak** them in water. Or use **stain remover**. Your mum has got stain remover, hasn't she?'

'I don't know,' I said quietly. Suddenly, I wanted the evening to finish.

'I'm really sorry,' I told Eline and Joy at the front door. I also wanted to say, 'I don't just mean about the carpet – I didn't mean to say you were boring.' But just then, I couldn't think of the right words.

'Don't worry,' said Eline. 'Thank you both for coming.' But her voice was not as warm as before.

spill (*past* **spilled, spilt**) to knock over by accident

soak to put in water for a long time

stain remover something that can clean very dirty clothes

33

READING CHECK

Put these sentences in the correct order.

a ☐ Jess and Violet go on a boat to see lots of places in Paris.

b ☐ When the girls leave, Eline's voice is not as warm as before.

c ☐ 1 Jess arrives in Paris.

d ☐ Violet looks at Eline's great photos.

e ☐ Violet and Jess walk to Eline and Joy's flat.

f ☐ Eline spills juice on Jess's jeans.

g ☐ Jess says that Violet thinks Eline and Joy are boring.

h ☐ Violet tells Eline and Joy that her dad died.

i ☐ Violet and Jess get ready to go out.

j ☐ They all eat dinner.

k ☐ Jess takes lots of photos of herself.

WORD WORK

1 Find seven more words from Chapter 5 in the letter square.

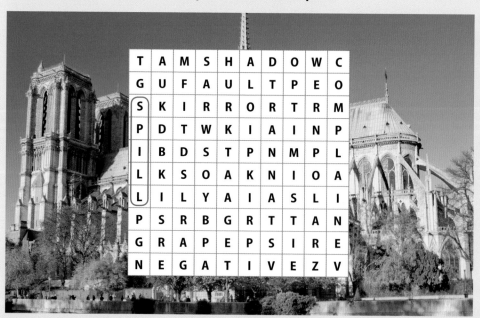

T	A	M	S	H	A	D	O	W	C
G	U	F	A	U	L	T	P	E	O
S	K	I	R	R	O	R	T	R	M
P	D	T	W	K	I	A	I	N	P
I	B	D	S	T	P	N	M	P	L
L	K	S	O	A	K	N	I	O	A
L	I	L	Y	A	I	A	S	L	I
P	S	R	B	G	R	T	T	A	N
G	R	A	P	E	P	S	I	R	E
N	E	G	A	T	I	V	E	Z	V

2 Complete the sentences using the words from Activity 1.

a It was my ...... fault ......, I dropped the coffee on the floor.

b My meal is cold and tastes bad, I am going to ....

c I'm hungry and thirsty – I would like a sandwich and some .... juice, please.

d I am always happy, so my friends say I am an ....

e I can't run for the train because I don't want to .... my coffee.

f It is too hot in the sun, let's sit in the .... of this tree instead.

g My brother can be so .... – I want him to be more positive!

h Oh no, there is chocolate on my coat – I will have to .... it in hot water.

GUESS WHAT

What happens next? Tick the boxes.

	Yes	No
a Jess throws her jeans in the bin.	☐	☐
b Violet wants to shout at Jess for being so rude.	☐	☐
c Violet's mum takes Jess to the airport in a boat.	☐	☐
d Violet feels bad about what Jess said to Eline and Joy.	☐	☐
e Jess sends Violet lots of messages on the way home.	☐	☐
f Violet's mum asks Jess if she wants to come and live with them in Paris.	☐	☐
g Jess cleans her jeans with stain remover and water.	☐	☐

6. Jess goes home

Back in my flat, Jess was soaking her jeans in some water. She was still really annoyed!

'You were right, Violet! Eline and Joy were so boring! I'm **almost** happy that I got juice on my jeans so we could leave! And Eline was so **rude**. She didn't even say sorry!'

I wanted to shout, 'You needed to say sorry! Not Eline!' Suddenly, I remembered that Jess was sometimes not very nice to people.

Jess looked at me. 'Don't look at me like that, Violet,' she said. 'You're the one who said they were boring.'

'But you didn't have to tell them,' I said.

Suddenly, Mum came in. 'Are you OK, girls? Jess, any luck with those jeans?'

Jess held up her jeans unhappily. I thought they looked clean.

'OK, well, goodnight,' said Mum. 'Don't stay up talking.'

In London, my mum always had to come in at 3 a.m. and tell us to stop talking! I thought that this time, we would talk all night. But actually, we just turned off the lights and went to sleep. Jess didn't even say thank you to my mum when we took her to the Eurostar station in a taxi.

It sounds bad, but I was almost **relieved** when Jess went home.

After Jess got the train, Mum said, 'Let's go for lunch!' So we went to Sacré-Cœur and had a chocolate *crepe* in a restaurant. Mum looked like she wanted to say something, but she didn't.

At last, in the taxi on the way home, Mum said, 'You didn't enjoy yourself with Jess, did you?'

'Yes, I did!' I said. OK, I didn't, but I didn't want Mum to say that. It sounded bad. Was she saying that we weren't best friends

almost nearly

rude not polite

relieved happy that something isn't a problem any more

36

anymore?

'Really?' asked Mum.

'One bad weekend doesn't mean we aren't still best friends,' I said angrily. 'You've never liked Jess!'

Mum said, 'I do like Jess! But I think you need to make some other friends, too. You need people that you spend time with every day at school, not just virtual friends that you talk to online.'

When she said that, we were driving past Eline and Joy's flat. I looked up at the fourth floor. They were my only friends in Paris, but after last night, everything felt wrong.

'Was it nice at Eline and Joy's flat?' asked Mum.

'I don't want to talk about it,' I said. I felt bad about last night.

The taxi arrived at our flat. Mum got some money and paid the driver. Then, silently, we walked into the building and went up in the lift.

'Violet, I don't understand you sometimes,' said Mum. 'Why won't you talk to me about anything?'

'Ha!' I said, before I could stop myself.

'What is it?' said Mum. We were at the top floor of the building and we went into the flat.

'I don't talk about anything?' I cried. 'What about you? You never talk about anything! You just pretend everything is fine.'

Mum looked surprised. She shut the door of the flat.

I turned to her and said, 'Then again, everything probably is fine, in your head! You're never unhappy about anything! You're never unhappy about – about Dad. You never even talk about him. All you care about is Paris and your job.'

Mum didn't look at me. Instead, she walked over to the window, with her back to me, and looked at the buildings outside. When she turned round, she was crying!

I felt terrible. I didn't want to **upset** her.

upset to make someone unhappy

Mum said, 'Violet, I think about your father all the time. OK? I'm sorry I don't talk about him. I find it too hard. And I don't want to make you unhappy. You don't talk about him either, you know?'

I looked away. I didn't want to think about it anymore. It was too difficult.

'You could talk about him,' Mum said quietly. 'Or you could think about him.'

Now I was crying. 'It's too hard,' I said. I looked down.

'Violet, look at me,' said Mum. 'I didn't have a **choice** about Paris.'

'What do you mean?'

'I didn't have a choice about Paris. OK? I had to take this job. It was either this job, or no job. The business is changing and some people are losing their jobs. I didn't tell you because I didn't want to worry you. Last year was so difficult for both of us.'

'But you said you really wanted to live in Paris!' I said.

'Well, I love Paris, that's true,' said Mum. 'But mostly we needed the money. We still need it, actually. You see, your father didn't leave us lots of money. So I needed to keep my job. And I thought perhaps there would be fewer sad **memories** here.'

I was silent while I thought about it. I felt like I didn't know anything.

Suddenly, the phone rang. I looked down. It was Jess! Why was she phoning me?

'Answer it!' said Mum.

'No, it's OK,' I said. It felt wrong to answer the phone while we were talking about this.

'Go on,' said Mum.

I walked into my bedroom. Actually, I knew why Jess was phoning. She wanted to say sorry. Our holiday was in September and it was only four weeks away. I was relieved. We needed to make things OK again before then.

'Hi, Jess,' I said into the phone.

'Violet,' said Jess, 'I want to talk to you about something.'

choice when you can choose or decide something

memories things you remember

38

READING CHECK

What do they say or think? Match the words to the people.

a Eline and Joy are so boring!

b You didn't enjoy yourself with Jess, did you?

c You never talk about Dad. All you care about is Paris and your job.

d You need to say sorry for being rude…

e I had to take this job!

f I know why Jess is phoning. She wants to say sorry.

1 thinks Violet when Jess phones.

2 Violet's mum tells Violet when they are in their flat.

3 says Jess when she is cleaning her jeans.

4 says Violet's mum in the taxi.

5 Violet thinks when she is with Jess in her flat after the dinner.

6 Violet tells her mum when they get home.

WORD WORK

1 Unscramble the words from Chapter 6.

a OSTALM
....almost.....

b DERU
....

c REVEDELI
....

d PSEUT
....

e ICCHOE
....

f MMORIESE
....

2 Fill in what Violet's mum is thinking with the words from Activity 1.

For a minute when I woke up this morning, I ....almost..... forgot that Violet and I are living in Paris now! I was .... because London had so many sad .... Moving to Paris was difficult but Starlight Cosmetics didn't really give me a .... Violet can be a little .... to me sometimes but I know she is just unhappy and .... about her dad and about leaving her friends.

GUESS WHAT

Which of these things do you think happen in the next chapter? Tick the boxes.

	Yes	No
a Violet packs her bag for her holiday in Spain.	☐	☐
b Jess tells Violet some bad news about Spain.	☐	☐
c Jess tells Violet she left her jeans in Paris.	☐	☐
d Violet's mum looks tired and unhappy.	☐	☐
e Violet's mum says her new job is too easy.	☐	☐
f Violet shouts at Jess about being so rude to Eline and Joy.	☐	☐

7. A surprise

'Danni?' I said, sitting down suddenly on my bed. 'You're going to Spain with Danni? Not me?'

'Yes,' said Jess.

'But – but you don't even like her that much,' I said, surprised. 'You said she was really boring and you wanted to put **jelly** in your ears instead of listening to her. And—'

'Don't say bad things about Danni,' said Jess. 'She's nice.'

Why was she suddenly being nice about Danni?

'OK,' I said slowly.

I began to ask myself, 'Do I really want Jess as my best friend?' Maybe I needed a cat, or something. Animals were much easier than people, weren't they? They were always nice to you. They weren't strange when they came to stay. And they didn't **invite** you on holiday and then take a different cat at the last minute.

'Oh, come on, Violet,' said Jess, suddenly annoyed. 'You left the country. It's been really hard for me too, you know.'

jelly a brightly coloured, sweet food that children eat in some countries

invite to ask someone to go to something with you

42

With Jess, everything was always other people's fault. If she walked on your foot, you needed to say sorry to her. So, yes, Jess gave my holiday place to Danni, but it was my fault because I went away.

'Why didn't you tell me while you were here?' I asked. Then I said, 'Oh. Is that why you came?'

Jess was silent.

'I'm sorry,' she said. 'There wasn't a good time to tell you.'

I was really angry. But I tried very hard not to shout. I told myself, 'You met Jess when you were both eight years old. She's just difficult sometimes.'

I **took a deep breath** and said, 'So – how's Danni? Is she still going to buy that hat, the same one that Lara bought?'

'Wait a minute,' said Jess. I could hear her asking something quietly. She wasn't talking to me. So who was she talking to? Then she came back.

'No,' said Jess. 'That hat was rubbish. Danni wants a different one now.'

'Jess,' I said angrily, 'is Danni there? Right now?'

'Yes,' said Jess. She sounded surprised by my question. 'But she needs to go home in a moment. Do you want to say hello? You're on **speakerphone**!'

'What?' I said angrily. She was talking to me about Danni while she was there, listening?

Suddenly, I was so angry that I put the phone down on Jess for the first time ever! It didn't feel like a big enough thing to do, so I **threw** the phone onto the wooden floor, too. The **screen** broke into lots of pieces.

Stupid French flats, I thought. No carpets. You can't even throw your phone onto the stupid floor and not break it. Stupid phone.

I picked it up. It was really broken. Now what could I do?

I sat alone in my room for a while, then went back into the living room. I wanted to talk to Mum.

take a deep breath to slowly take in lots of air through your mouth or nose, usually to stop yourself from feeling angry or upset

speakerphone when everyone in the room can hear the person talking on your phone

throw (past **threw, thrown**) to push something quickly through the air with your hands

screen the flat, glass front of a TV, computer, or phone

She was sitting at the table. It was starting to get dark. In this
light, she suddenly looked old and tired.

'How did I not see this?' I asked myself. Then I thought,
'I didn't see this because I've only thought about myself.'

'Shall I turn on your special French light for you?' I asked
Mum.

Mum almost smiled.

'I'm sorry about earlier,' I said. 'I didn't mean what I said
about Dad.'

'It's OK,' said Mum.

'You said your job in London was in trouble... but the job here
is OK, right?'

Mum was quiet. 'Well, if you really want me to tell you
everything...'

'I do,' I said.

'Then, no, it isn't going very well.'

'Oh,' I said slowly. Here was another thing that I didn't see before. I thought of all the evenings when Mum wore her old clothes on the sofa. And she always looked tired because she wasn't sleeping well.

'What's wrong?' I asked.

'I need ideas,' said Mum. 'Ideas for some new make-up. It's not giving names to things. This time, I need to decide how the photos will look. I have to think of something new by tomorrow. They didn't like my first ideas.'

'What were your first ideas?' I asked.

'I wanted to take photos of the make-up by different famous places in Paris. The Eiffel Tower, Sacré-Cœur... but they said it was too boring and it wasn't a new idea.'

'Can I help?' I said, like this was an American film and I could make everything OK by running through busy traffic, going into her office and **delighting** a room full of business people with my great ideas.

'No, it's fine,' said Mum. 'I'm tired, but I'll probably feel better in a minute. Perhaps I just need some chocolate.'

Mum looked really tired, just then. She didn't look excited. I wasn't sure that even chocolate was the answer.

Suddenly, Mum saw my broken phone.

'Oh no! Your screen! What happened?' she asked.

I looked down at the broken phone in my hand. My phone was once the most important thing I had. It was the only way I could talk to my old world. Now the screen was in pieces. Strangely, I didn't care that much.

'Don't worry,' I said. 'Shall I get you some chocolate from the cupboard?'

'No, it's OK, Violet,' said Mum. 'Go out for five minutes. Have a walk. I'll try to think of new ideas.'

'Are you sure?' I said.

'Yes. Go!' said Mum.

'OK,' I said. 'There's something I need to do.'

delight to make very happy

45

READING CHECK

Complete these sentences with the correct names. You can use each name more than once.

Violet

Violet's mum

Jess

Eline

Danni

a ......*Jess*....... is suddenly being nice about ..... *Danni*......!

b .... tells .... she is going to Spain with ....

c .... thinks, 'do I really want .... as my best friend?'

d .... is angry because .... tells her that .... is in the room listening to them talking!

e .... throws her phone on the floor and it breaks.

f .... looks tired and says that her job is not going well.

g .... needs some new ideas by Monday.

h .... says she is going out because there is something she needs to do.

WORD WORK

Use the correct form of the words in the broken phone to complete the sentences. You can use each word more than once.

invite

jelly

take a deep breath

speakerphone

delight

throw

screen

a After dinner, children in some countries like eating ...... *jelly* ....

b Oh no – I've broken the .... of my TV!

c When they gave me my birthday present, I was really ....

d I will .... her to the party.

e Jess was making me really angry. I slowly ....

f I .... the ball.

g She didn't know she was on .... and everyone could hear her!

h Once, when I was a child, I ate lots and lots of .... , then felt very sick.

i I .... bottles of water at the crowd, because I knew they were thirsty.

j I hope he .... me to the party because I really want to go.

GUESS WHAT

What happens next? Tick the boxes.

a ☐ Violet buys a new phone.

b ☐ Violet's mum thinks of some good ideas.

c ☐ Violet goes to see Eline.

d ☐ Danni phones Violet's mum and shouts at her.

e ☐ Violet buys her mum an umbrella.

f ☐ Violet's mum runs away because she is unhappy.

8. Real friends

'This is for you,' I said to Eline. I was at the door of her flat.

She looked surprised to see me.

'I'm sorry I didn't call before I came,' I said. 'My phone's broken.'

'Oh no!' said Eline.

'It's OK,' I said. 'Perhaps it's not that important.'

Eline looked down at the stain remover. I bought it from the shop on the way to her flat. I needed to do a lot of **miming** to explain what I wanted in French.

'It's to clean the carpet,' I said. 'I'm really sorry about the other night.'

'Come in,' said Eline.

I went inside.

'Is Joy at home?' I asked.

'No, she's at the park,' said Eline.

Oh dear. The white carpet was gone.

Eline saw me looking. 'White was a stupid colour for a carpet,' she said.

mime to talk
with your hands

'I'm really sorry,' I said.

'It wasn't your fault,' said Eline.

'Well, I'm sorry about what Jess said.'

'It's OK,' said Eline.

'No, it's not,' I said. 'It was true. I said – I said that you were boring when I first moved here. But it was before I knew you. I don't think you're boring. Actually, I was the boring one. I was always on my phone.'

'Don't worry about it,' said Eline. She smiled. 'Would you like a drink?'

'Just water,' I said carefully.

Eline laughed.

I waited in her front room and looked around at all the nice things. Eline's photos were on the wall. They really were very good.

When Eline walked back into the room, I was standing by the door. I was excited, but I was trying to hide it.

'What is it?' she asked.

'Eline, what are you doing for the next few hours?'

An hour later, Eline, Mum, and I were all sitting around the table in my flat. We had lots of make-up and photos in front of us.

We all looked at our pens and our pieces of paper. My paper was empty. So was Mum's. Eline's had a picture of a star.

'What about just taking photos of the nail polish?' I said.

'I've tried that already,' said Mum. 'But the people at work want something behind the bottles of nail polish... what about photo **frames**?'. We could put each nail polish in a frame.'

'Perhaps,' I said.

'What about Paris?' said Eline.

Mum looked down. Eline didn't know about Mum's earlier idea of Paris – the idea that didn't work.

'People have used photos of Paris so many times before – the old buildings, the beautiful streets,' said Mum quietly. 'The idea just didn't work when I tried it before. It's all **a bit** old.'

frame the square piece of wood outside a picture

a bit a little

'Maybe look at Paris differently?' said Eline.

'What do you mean?' asked Mum.

'I don't know,' said Eline. She thought about it for a second, then said, 'I like taking photos of a strange place where **artists** work, near the river. It's called Les Frigos. It's an old building, full of **graffiti**, so there are lots of different colours to photograph. It's Paris, but it's really different. Paris is more than old buildings and the Eiffel Tower.'

Mum paused. Then she started writing on her piece of paper. 'That's a great idea. I like it! We can write, 'You thought you knew make-up? Look again.' Or, 'Make-up – think again."

'Also,' said Eline, 'you could take photos at the beach!'

'The beach?' I said. 'I thought this idea was about Paris?'

Eline saw my face. 'I know Paris isn't by the sea, but there's a beach here!' said Eline. 'Every summer, they make a beach by the river. They bring in **sand**, just for four weeks! So, you could take a photo of some make-up on the sand with the old buildings and the river behind. But of course, you aren't really by the sea, you're still in Paris.'

artist a person who makes pictures

graffiti writing or painting on a wall, usually in the street

sand it is yellow and we find a lot of it on the beach

50

'That's good!' said Mum. She sounded excited. 'You know, I think I can use this. I just need to work on it a bit more.'

Eline and I went to sit on the sofa while Mum wrote at the table. She was writing fast. She always wrote fast when she was happy.

'I was thinking, I've got an old phone you can have if you like,' said Eline.

'Oh – that's nice of you!' I said.

'But it only makes calls in France. Phone calls to London don't work. Actually, if you call London more than once a fortnight, it **explodes**.'

I think she was joking.

Thirty minutes later, Mum said that she was finished.

'I'll finish it in the morning and then show it to the people at work!' she said. 'Thanks, Eline!'

'Any time,' said Eline. 'Violet, shall I come round with that phone tomorrow? But only if you want me to.'

'Yes please,' I said, and smiled.

'So, this is English chocolate,' I told Eline and Joy.

It was a week later, and we were standing in my kitchen. We were trying some of the English food that I brought with me.

explode to break open suddenly with a very loud noise

Mum came into the kitchen.

'Eline, this is to say thank you,' she said. She gave Eline a big bag full of Starlight Cosmetics make-up!

'Wow – are you sure? Thank you!' said Eline. 'Joy – look!'

'It went really well at work,' said Mum. 'And it was because of you and Violet.'

'She means you,' I told Eline.

'I talked about the ideas,' Mum told Eline, 'and everybody liked them! The other marketing people all got very excited and started thinking about other new places in Paris that they could use. It was great!'

'So, they gave you a new job and lots more money?' I said optimistically.

'No,' said Mum. 'But I feel much better. I think the people at work are happy. This will be good for me.'

I already knew that things were better, because Mum was sleeping well again at night.

'Are you three going out or not?' asked Mum.

'Yes!' said Eline. 'We have to do some interesting things before we start school again!'

'What are you going to do?' asked Mum.

I smiled. 'We're going to walk round Paris – that's Eline's idea – then see an English film. That's my idea! Then we'll come home for food, if that's OK?'

'Ha!' said Mum happily.

'What?' I said.

'You just called the flat home,' she replied.

'No, I didn't,' I said.

'Yes, you did!' she laughed. 'Does that mean you like it here now?'

I laughed too. 'Well... I still think a place is all about the people. But now I like the people, too. So, yes, it's home.'

explore to walk around a new place and learn about it

Eline, Joy, and I walked towards the door of the flat. The sun was very bright outside. It was a nice day to go out and **explore**. At last, I thought I was going to be happy here in Paris.

READING CHECK

Are these sentences true or false?

		True	False
a	Violet gives Eline a sandwich.	☐	☑
b	Violet tells Jess that she is really boring.	☐	☐
c	Eline takes really good photos.	☐	☐
d	Eline says that she knows a strange building that is covered in graffiti.	☐	☐
e	Violet, Eline, and Joy try some Norwegian food in Violet's kitchen.	☐	☐
f	Violet's mum gives Eline a drink of water to say thank you.	☐	☐
g	Starlight Cosmetics liked Violet's mum's new ideas.	☐	☐
h	Violet now says that Paris is her home!	☐	☐

WORD WORK

1 Match the words with the definitions.

a	mime	1	to look around a place that you don't know yet
b	frame	2	person who makes things or paints pictures
c	artist	3	to talk with your hands
d	a bit	4	a thing made from wood that holds a picture
e	Les Frigos	5	writing on a wall with paint, done without someone saying it is OK
f	graffiti	6	to open up very quickly all by itself, usually making a loud noise
g	explode	7	a little
h	explore	8	an unusual building in Paris where lots of artists work

2 Correct the sentences using the correct form of the words from Activity 1.

a We don't speak the same language so I have to ~~fly~~  mime to explain what I mean.

b It is a beautiful picture; I am going to put it in a cupboard . . . .

c Stella's paintings are beautiful; she is a very good postman . . . .

d People sometimes paint sheep . . . . on the wall at night.

e I really like to call . . . . places that I don't know yet.

f We have to get out of here; the building is going to crash . . . .!

GUESS WHAT

What do you think happens after the story ends? Choose from these ideas or add your own.

a ☐ Violet, Eline, and Joy work hard at the international school.

b ☐ Eline gets a job at Starlight Cosmetics.

c ☐ Jess and Danni argue a lot in Spain.

d ☐ Starlight Cosmetics gives Violet's mum a job in New York.

e ☐ Violet buys Eline and Joy a new white carpet.

f ☐ Violet puts lots of photos online of her, Eline, and Joy having fun.

g ☐ Violet tells everyone how much she loves Paris.

h ☐ . . . .

i ☐ . . . .

Project A *Places in Paris*

1 **Here are some of Jess's photos of Paris. Match the descriptions to the places.**

1 The .... is very tall. When people think of it, they think of Paris. It is famous all over the world. It was built from 1887–1889 and is 300.65 metres high.

2 .... is a big white church. It is on a hill in the north of Paris. You have to climb lots of steps to get there. Lots of people like to visit it and look at the view.

3 .... is another very famous church in Paris. It was built between 1163–1345. It is next to the river. It is famous for its beautiful coloured glass windows.

2 **Eline tells Violet and her mum about some great places in Paris that are not as famous as the Eiffel Tower or Sacré-Cœur. Fill in the gaps using the words from the box.**

> Old   unusual   beautiful   summer   sand
> river   cheap   graffiti   building

1 Les Frigos is an .... place in Paris. It is a .... where artists live and work. Few tourists know about it. It has lots of .... on the inside and outside. It is not open to tourists but if you ask very nicely it is sometimes possible to visit and take photographs.

2 The Paris beach is only there in the .... There is lots of .... so it looks like a real beach. People can rest, play games, or read near the ....

3 The flea market is a good place to buy .... things. Some of the things that people sell are very .... and ....

3 Read this online comment from someone who owns a small restaurant near one of the famous places in Paris. Fill in the table below.

Paris gets so many visitors from other countries – more every year! So many people come here on holiday. They stand still in the street instead of walking along. They take hundreds of photos of themselves in front of the Eiffel Tower. And when they come into my restaurant, sometimes they just sit down without saying anything! In France, it is important to always say good morning or good afternoon when you enter someone's restaurant!

Then again, my son tells me to be more positive. People are always happy to be in Paris, and say it is a beautiful city. They spend money in our restaurant, and when they pay the bill, they often leave extra money for my son.

It's funny: people think French people spend all day drinking coffee outside their favourite restaurant, but most people who live in Paris are too busy for that! Our business does well because of visitors. So maybe I need to say thank you to them.

What does the writer think of visitors to Paris? Fill in the table with the pros and cons.

Pros	Cons

4 Describe a place in your town to a partner. What do you like and dislike about it?

Project B *Emails Home*

1 Read the email and answer the questions.

From: rose@parismail.oup.com   1 August, 00:17am

Dear Laura,

I'm sorry I haven't written before. It has been really busy since we moved here to Paris. Paris is beautiful. The flat is small but it has big windows and a lovely view.

My new job is very busy. I don't think I am doing very well, but I need this job! I am not sleeping very well. When I get home, I am so tired that all I want to do is lie on the sofa.

I am trying to help Violet make new friends, but she seems so unhappy. She is on her phone a lot.

I miss David a lot. I feel so alone sometimes. You must miss him too – he was your brother! I keep thinking about our old life in London. It was so perfect: David, me and Violet, all together. I told him it was dangerous to cycle to work every day, with all those cars and buses. But he still did it because he loved cycling. He was always positive and never afraid. And now I have to be positive about everything, too, for Violet.

Let me know all your news.

Love

Rose x

Who is the person writing the email?

Violet's uncle / Violet's friend Laura / Violet's mum / Violet's teacher

Who is the email for?

Violet's dad / Violet's aunt / Violet's best friend / Violet's cousin

Who is David?

Violet's teacher / Violet's grandfather / Violet's dad / Violet's uncle

How does the person writing the letter feel? *(Circle more than one)*

happy / tired / busy / excited / sad / alone

What does the person like about their flat? *(Circle more than one)*

the cost / the view / the kitchen / the carpets / the big windows / the light

2 Read the email and use the words in the box to fill in the blanks.

| annoying | fault | friends | jeans | photos | nail varnish |
| beach | alone | holiday | boring | told | Spain |

From: jess@shopping.oup.com

25 September, 16:30

Dear Violet,

How are you? I know we haven't spoken since I . . . . you about Danni coming to . . . . with me instead of you. Don't be angry with me. I'm sorry, but it's not my . . . . you moved away, is it?

The . . . . in Spain was terrible. Danni ate some bad food and she was in bed for lots of the week. It was terrible for me because I had to sit on the . . . . with my mum and dad while she was sick. It was so . . . .

How is the international school? I feel very sorry for you, all . . . . without me there. Who will you be . . . . with? Those girls, Eline and Joy? I was very upset about my . . . . ! I don't wear them any more now because Ruby bought the same ones. It was so . . . . !

The only good thing about Spain is that I took some great . . . . of myself – did you see them online?

If you want to be friends again, please could you send me some more Starlight Cosmetics make-up? My . . . . has all gone and I need some more.

Thanks!

Love

Jess xxx

3 Imagine you have moved to a new country. Write a list using the table below.

Things I miss	Things I am excited about

4 Now write an email to your old friends about how you feel living in the new country. Use the things from your table.

GRAMMAR CHECK

Verbs of Perception

We use the verbs feel, look, and sound to describe perception.

We use feel + adjective to talk about feelings on the inside.

I feel cold.

We use look or sound + adjective to talk about how things are on the outside.

The grape juice looked dark against the white carpet.

The music sounded loud.

The past tense of the verb to feel is irregular.

I felt sad when I thought how happy we were in London.

1 **Complete Violet's email to Jess with the correct form of the verb in brackets. Think about whether you need the present or past tense.**

Hi Jess,

How are you? I miss you! Everyone said moving to Paris ...*sounded*... (sound) wonderful, but actually being here is different. I .... (feel) very unhappy. All the students who were at the international school party .... (look) boring. I met one girl, Eline. Mum saw us talking. She said hello to Eline and .... (sound) really excited! But all I .... (feel) was that no one can replace my friends from home.

I saw your photos online of the clothes you were wearing last weekend. They .... (look) new. Did you all go shopping? The long coat .... (look) beautiful. In the photo, it .... (look) brown – or is it black? When I saw the photos, I .... (feel) happy that you had a nice day. But I also .... (feel) sad that I wasn't there!

I must go. Mum said I use my phone too much. She .... (sound) annoyed.

Violet x

GRAMMAR CHECK

Past Continuous and Past Simple

We use the Past Simple for finished past events.

We use the Past Continuous for an activity that was in progress when events in the Past Simple happened.

We use was / were + present participle to make the Past Continuous.

We often use when to introduce the Past Simple verb and while to introduce the Past Continuous verb.

I was carrying a box of heavy books when Mum said, 'Look at these beautiful stairs!'

Mum said, 'Look at these beautiful stairs!' while I was carrying a box of heavy books.

2 Complete the sentences with the Past Continuous or Past Simple form of the verbs in brackets.

a I ...... *sat* ...... (sit) on the sofa while the men .. *were helping* .. (help) us move.

b At the international school party, Mum .... (smile) at everyone while I .... (feel) embarrassed.

c I .... (get) a drink when I .... (meet) Eline.

d I .... (walk) over the bridge when I .... (send) Jess a message on my phone.

e I .... (sit) with Mum in the park when Eline .... (say), 'Hi!'

f I .... (feel) really happy when Mum .... (tell) me the news about Jess's visit.

GRAMMAR CHECK

Comparative / Superlative adjectives

We use a comparative adjective + than to say that two people or things are different in some way.

Joy is younger than Eline.   *Eline and Joy's flat is bigger than Violet's flat.*

	Comparative	Superlative
most short adjectives	add -er *young – younger*	add the + -est *the youngest*
adjectives that finish in -e	add -r *safe – safer*	add the + -st *the safest*
adjectives that finish in a consonant + y	change the -y to -i and add -er *easy – easier*	change the -y to -i and add the + -est *the easiest*
adjectives that finish in a short vowel + consonant	double the consonant and add -er *hot – hotter*	double the consonant and add the + -est *the hottest*
adjectives of three syllables or more	put more before the adjective *difficult – more difficult*	add the most *the most difficult*

3 Complete the gaps in the sentences.

a Eline is ..... older ..... (old) than her sister Joy.

b Joy is the .... (young) in their family.

c Violet is .... (sad) than her mum at leaving London.

d Violet's mum looks .... (happy) than Violet.

e Jess is Violet's .... (cool) friend.

4 Complete the gaps in the sentences using *more than* or *most*.

a Violet misses all her friends, but she misses Jess the ....

b Violet's mum likes Paris .... Violet.

c Violet thinks her mum is the .... embarrassing person she knows.

d At first, Violet says Eline is even .... boring .... Maisie Bickford.

e Violet is .... negative about Paris .... her mum.

GRAMMAR

GRAMMAR CHECK

Adverbs of manner

We use adverbs of manner to talk about how we do things.

We make adverbs from adjectives by adding -ly

Mum shook me excitedly.

For adjectives that end in -y, we change y to -ily

'Is Danni there?' I said angrily.

5 Combine the two phrases using the correct adverb.

a 'I miss your dad,' said Mum. She was sad.

'I miss your dad,' said Mum sadly.

b I walked home behind Mum. I was slow.

....

c I put down the phone. I felt unhappy.

....

d I tried to clean the rug. I was quick.

....

e 'My jeans!' cried Jess. She was angry.

....

f I hugged Mum. I was happy!

....

GRAMMAR CHECK

Conditional Sentences

We use if + Present Simple + *will* future to talk about the results of a possible situation.

If you don't reply, I will feel alone.

We use if + Present Simple + imperative to tell or ask someone to do something in a possible situation.

If you want to enjoy Paris, stop looking at your phone all the time.

The if clause can come at the start or the end of the sentence. When it comes at the start, we put a comma after it.

If you think I'm boring, just tell me.

6 **Complete Eline's email to Violet with the correct form of the verbs in the box.**

be	come	feel	help	leave	miss
move	remember	~~send~~	show	want	

From: eline@parismail.oup.com

Hi Violet,

I haven't known you for very long, so I don't know if I will ...... *send* ...... this email. If you really don't .... to make any new friends in Paris, I will .... you alone. But I know how you feel because I remember how it felt when Joy and I .... here from Norway. If you want to .... happy, try to make some new friends! And if you .... lonely, ... that there are lots of nice people here. If you want, I can .... you meet other students at the international school. I know everyone!

.... to my flat tomorrow afternoon if you like. I can .... you some great photos of your new class at school. But if you don't want to, I understand. Sometimes it takes a while to stop .... your old friends. But if you need a new friend, I'm here.

From

Eline

GRAMMAR CHECK

Participle phrases

In stories, we often talk about two actions that happen at the same time.

'Are you OK?' said Eline. She looked at me.

If the subject is the same for both verbs, it often sounds better to make one sentence. We add a comma after the first verb phrase, then use the -ing form of the second verb.

'Are you OK?' said Eline, looking at me.

7   Use participle phrases to combine the pairs of sentences.

a   We stood in the kitchen. We tried some English chocolate.
   We stood in the Kitchen, trying some English chocolate.

b   'That's a great idea!' said Mum. She wrote something on her paper.

....

c   'Hello!' said my mum. She smiled at Eline.

....

d   'What's the film about?' I asked. I looked at the TV.

....

e   'Good for her', said Mum. She watched the film.

....

f   Eline stood in front of us. She held a camera.

....

g   'You hated London!' said Jess. She laughed.

....

h   'You're going to Spain with Danni?' I said. I sat down suddenly on my bed.

....

i   'I need to buy stain remover,' I said. I mimed to show what I wanted.

....

GRAMMAR CHECK

Talking about the future

We use *will*, *going to*, and the Present Continuous to talk about the future.

When we think about a plan before we speak, we use *going to* or the Present Continuous.

'I'm going to visit Paris to see you, Violet.'

'We're seeing lots of old buildings this afternoon.'

We often use the Present Continuous to talk about things in the future that are *already organized*.

We use will to talk about decisions we make *at the moment* of speaking.

'I'll take a photo!' said Jess when she saw the old bridge.

8 Complete what the characters are thinking.

How . . . . I tell Violet I want Danni to come to Spain instead of her? I know, ... phone her when I get home. But she is . . . . be angry. . . . . tell her it's not my fault. She moved away, not me!

Jess

What am I . . . . do at the international school? Who am I . . . . talk to? . . . . it be terrible without Jess?

Violet

. . . . Starlight Cosmetics like the new ideas? . . . . my job be safe after this? . . . . tell them the new ideas tomorrow morning. Or . . . . I wait until the weekly meeting in the afternoon? If they like my ideas, I'm . . . . be so happy! I know, ... give Eline some make-up to say thank you. She is . . . . like that, I think.

Violet's mum

DOMINOES Your Choice

Read *Dominoes* for pleasure, or to develop language skills. It's your choice.

Each *Domino* reader includes:
- a good story to enjoy
- integrated activities to develop reading skills and increase vocabulary
- task-based projects – perfect for CEFR portfolios
- contextualized grammar activities

Each *Domino* pack contains a reader, and an excitingly dramatized audio recording of the story

If you liked this Level Two *Domino*, read these:

Who am I?
Or, the Modern Frankenstein
Emma Howell

Vic has no friends. Everyone else has friends, and it makes him angry. So, Vic makes a new name for himself online, so he can make other people feel the way he does. But soon Vic finds it difficult to control what he has created…

Will Vic's mistake hurt people, or can he stop it in time? What will happen to Vic? And what will happen to the monster he has made?

Jemma's Jungle Adventure
Anne Collins

Jemma is very excited when she joins an expedition to the island of Kamora. She hopes to learn about doing scientific research, and to find a very rare bird of paradise.

She is happy to meet the famous Dr Malone and the wise Dr Al Barwani, and to help to research birds, snakes, and insects. But things start to go wrong. Someone has a terrible secret, and there is danger for Jemma – and for the bird.

Who has a secret plan, and what is it? What will happen to the bird? And what will happen to Jemma?

	CEFR	Cambridge Exams	IELTS	TOEFL iBT	TOEIC
Level 3	B1	PET	4.0	57-86	550
Level 2	A2–B1	KET-PET	3.0-4.0	–	390
Level 1	A1–A2	YLE Flyers/KET	3.0	–	225
Starter & Quick Starter	A1	YLE Movers	1.0–2.0	–	–

You can find details and a full list of books and teachers' resources on our website: www.oup.com/elt/gradedreaders